CHRISTMAS PUZZLES

Publications International, Ltd.

Brain Games is a registered trademark of Publications International, Ltd.

Additional images from Shutterstock.com

Copyright © 2025 Publications International, Ltd. All rights reserved. This book may not be reproduced or quoted in whole or in part by any means whatsoever without written permission from:

Louis Weber, CEO
Publications International, Ltd.
8140 Lehigh Avenue
Morton Grove, IL 60053

Permission is never granted for commercial purposes.

ISBN: 978-1-63938-894-3

Manufactured in China.

8 7 6 5 4 3 2 1

Let's get social!

📷 @Publications_International

📘 @PublicationsInternational

📘 @BrainGames.TM

www.pilbooks.com

'Tis the Season to be Puzzling

Brain Games Christmas Puzzles features a wide variety of festive challenges to engage your brain. Inside you'll find over 100 anagrams, crosswords, cryptograms, quizzes, word searches, and more—all holiday-themed to keep you in the Christmas spirit!

Decode bits of holiday trivia from around the world, or complete the Christmas quote from beloved American figures like cartoonist Charles Schulz. Match the classic carol title to its singer, or piece together tiles to reveal a Christmas picture.

From the classic holiday traditions that go back several generations, to the pop carols heard over the radio, **Brain Games Christmas Puzzles** promises to deliver on some festive fun! If you find yourself stuck, answers can be found in the back of the book.

Pop Quiz

The poem now known as "'Twas the Night Before Christmas" was first published under this title.

A. "The Night Before Christmas"
B. "Account of a Visit from St. Nicholas"
C. "A Visit from St. Nicholas"
D. It was left untitled.

Answer on page 106.

Oh What Fun

Cryptograms are messages in substitution code. Break the code to read the message. For example, THE SMART CAT might become FVO QWGDF JGF if F is substituted for T, V for H, O for E, and so on.

MEYON "BYRVON INOOK" ZYVEQ IN PRN PU QEN ZPKQ

WNGPVRYHXION GEWYKQZXK QFRNK PU XOO QYZN, QEN KPRV

MXK PWYVYRXOOS MWYQQNR IS BXZNK OPWC DYNWDPRQ QP

GNONIWXQN QEXRLKVYJYRV. YQ MXK YRYQYXOOS QYQONC

"QEN PRN EPWKN DNR KONYVE."

Answer on page 106.

Star Power

Fill each of the squares in the grid so that every green star is surrounded by a digit from 1 to 8 with no repeats.

Answers on page 106.

O Is for Ornaments

Every word listed is contained within the group of letters. Words can be found in a straight line horizontally, vertically, or diagonally. They may be read either forward or backward.

OATMEAL
OCCASION
OFFICE PARTY
OLAF
OLIVE
ONCE
OPENING
OPULENT
ORANGES
ORNAMENTS
OUTREACH
OVATION
OVEN
OVERCOAT
OWL
OXEN

```
Y N I N E P O D O O C C A S I O
O F F I C G P A R E O V I L O T
O P U L E N T P G H N L D H N O
D U N C N O F N C C U N I E R E
O X E O A M A A I E O B M V X C
O T L R L R E F M I L A L O E O
C N U N O R F T S O N C T A V V
C E P A T O A A V R A F S L O A
M V L U T O C I O E A T G O R T
O O O J A C L N R L N N M V A I
V W G K O O W T O E I S C E Z O
O E L X C U U O M N N R N A A N
X Y O O R O O A E C N O O V H L
E A A P E L N P G V E R C O A N
N Q T U V R O X E O R A N G E S
E V O L O F F I C E P A R T Y Y
```

Answers on page 106.

Bundle Up

Change just one letter on each line to go from the top word to the bottom word. Do not change the order of the letters. You must have a common English word at each step.

COLD

_____

_____ accompanies a gift

_____

WARM

Answers on page 107.

Either/Or

Complete the sentence with two words that are anagrams of each other (e.g. CARE and RACE).

On Christmas Eve, the family gathers to ____ stories by the hearth while everyone ____ the fire crackling.

Answers on page 107.

North Pole

Using the following list of clues, find words of four or five letters hidden in the phrase **NORTH POLE**.

1. Fill-in option on surveys, often ____
2. Word before student or roll ____
3. Stem hazard ____
4. Rescuer ____
5. Christmas or a carol ____
6. "SOS!" ____
7. Not yep ____
8. Well-versed in verse ____
9. A French instrumental wreath? ____
10. Accommodating place ____
11. Kids skip it ____
12. Backstory or folk knowledge ____

Answers on page 107.

Red and Green

ACROSS
1. Culinary concoction
5. Bubbly drink
9. Viewpoint
14. Sudden inspiration
15. Big birds Down Under
16. Poops out
17. Santa's ride
19. Root veggies
20. Earmark
21. Make a decision
22. Walk to and fro
23. Heavy hammer
25. Feigns
29. Humanitarian organization
31. Beat walker
32. Burns wildly
35. Come to a stop
36. Sensible
37. Miscalculates
38. Seethes
39. Small, brown bird
40. Stage signals
41. More than that
42. Took on, as cargo
43. Bart Simpson's grandpa
44. Packers' home
46. Carolina team
48. Solution
52. Tango teams
53. Tax-deferred letters
54. Chopping tool
55. Buenos ___, Argentina
57. Stop commands
60. Type of target shooting
61. Burn balm
62. Yesteryear
63. Mary-Louise Parker Showtime hit
64. Skillfully deceptive
65. Castle ringer

DOWN
1. Loam, loess, etc.
2. Absolutely perfect
3. Marsh grass
4. Possesses
5. Oozed
6. Fail to include
7. Used shovels
8. Volcanic residue
9. Plate appearances
10. Reunion attendee
11. Alien's permission to work
12. Give permission to
13. 19th letter
18. Forward sections of mezzanines
22. Nuisances
24. Garb for a girl
25. Lauds
26. Deodorant option
27. Transplant recipient
28. Use credit

30. Irritability
32. Hit the high points
33. Island in the Antilles
34. Ornament home?
36. Vacillates
38. Exposes
42. Veranda in Hawaii
44. Spirits
45. Cereal grass
47. Winter wool
49. Yippee!
50. Beyond requirements
51. VCR button
53. Golden calf, for one
55. Naval warfare branch: abbr.
56. President's nickname
57. Untrained
58. Yale grad
59. Exercise site

Answers on page 107.

Matching

Match each holiday greeting to the language it comes from.

1. Buon Natale
2. God Jul
3. Vrolijk kerstfeest
4. Feliz Natal

A. Dutch
B. Portuguese
C. Italian
D. Swedish

Answers on page 107.

C_ndy _nd M_r_

Below is a list of holiday treats, but they lost the vowels A, E, I, O, and U, as well as any punctuation and spaces between words. Can you figure out the missing vowels and name each treat in the list below?

1. PNTBRTTL
2. CHCLTRNG
3. CNDDNTS
4. PCNPRLN
5. SLTDCRML
6. CHCLTTRFFL
7. BTTRTFF
8. CRMLPPCRN

Answers on page 107.

Star Power

Fill each of the squares in the grid so that every green star is surrounded by a digit from 1 to 8 with no repeats.

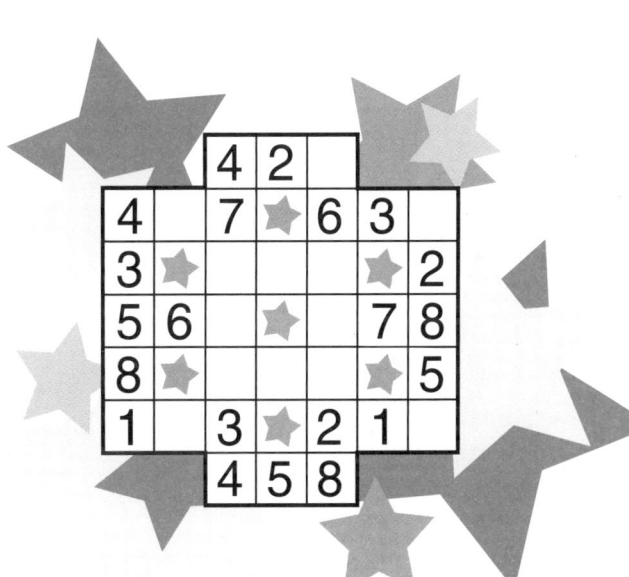

Answers on page 108.

The Nutcracker

BALLET
CHRISTMAS EVE
CLARA
CLOCK
COURT
DANCER
DOLL
DREAM
FAIRY
FLOWER
FRITZ

MOUSE KING
NUTCRACKER
OWL
PINE FOREST
PRINCE
SNOWFLAKE
SOLDIER
STAHLBAUM
SUGAR PLUM
TCHAIKOVSKY
WALTZ

```
A A E F D A R A L C Z Z Z H W O
B L K D M U L P R A G U S L E E
S F A I A W D E D K G W X O V M
T R L M E C E B C S D A N C E R
A I F B R E W O L F G N M N S G
H T W B P B L O T R U O C U A H
L Z O A K C A J M B P A H T M T
B W N L Y K S V O K I A H C T F
A E S L A R M R U Q N B E R S P
U R O E F A C E S W E Q C A I J
M B W T E E P I E T F H N C R X
K Z L R W H U D K Y O A I K H U
Q Y D Z D Q L L I R R G R E C Y
O C E O H L Q O N I E E P R O B
B P K N O B P S G A S V X W G S
R W F D O U M W A F T W A L T Z
```

Answers on page 108.

Toys for Tykes

Change just one letter on each line to go from the top word to the bottom word. Do not change the order of the letters. You must have a common English word at each step.

TRAIN

____

____

____

TRUCK

Answers on page 108.

Either/Or

Complete the sentence with two words that are anagrams of each other (e.g. CARE and RACE).

____ spent with family or friends are special ____ to enjoy during the holiday season.

Answers on page 108.

Santa Claus

Using the following list of clues, find words of four or five letters hidden in the phrase SANTA CLAUS.

1. Gondolier's road ____
2. Young lady ____
3. Soft, fine mineral ____
4. Steam bath ____
5. Elegance ____
6. Sparse ____
7. CT or MRI ____
8. Fish in melts and cans ____
9. Tribe ____
10. Saucy dance? ____
11. Give a part to play ____
12. Pretends ____

Answers on page 108.

Winter Blues

ACROSS
1. Formers of man-made lakes
5. "First, do no ___"
9. Send, as payment
10. Rap sheet word
12. Winter ___ (home of the Czars)
13. Winter ___ (luge, et al.)
15. Jed Clampett's discovery
16. Proofreaders' marks
18. Ill humor
19. Super-secure airline
21. Nondairy milk source
22. Irish or Manx speaker
23. School attended by 007
25. Prison-related
26. Winter ___ (Florida site of Cypress Gardens amusement park)
28. Rest period
29. Dynamite inventor Alfred
30. Vientiane's land
31. "... or ___!" (threat ender)
32. Long-snouted swimmer
33. Active European volcano
37. Eng. major's course
38. California mandarin
40. Hi-___ graphics
41. Winter ___ (place to play instructional ball)
43. Winter ___ (starchy vegetable)
45. Laugh-a-minute folks
46. Goes bad
47. Thomas, creator of the Republican elephant
48. Has a bug

DOWN
1. Mason aide Street
2. Org. with a famous journal
3. Boom box plug-ins
4. Cowboy topper
5. In a rush
6. Barrier crossed by Hannibal
7. Carnival city
8. ___ Islands (Guam's group)
9. One way to travel
11. Ripken's record, e.g.
12. "The Tell-Tale Heart" writer
14. Bear's advice
17. Seemingly forever
20. Flood zone sight
22. Fliers in skeins
24. Gas additive
25. Tennis club figure
26. More moth-eaten
27. Choose not to vote
28. Starbucks worker
29. Jodie Foster title role
30. Long. crosser
32. B&B visitor
34. ___ fats

35. Top "Untouchable"
36. Bat wood
38. Removes from the roster
39. Prefix with distant or lateral
42. ___ few rounds (spar)
44. It may be bookmarked

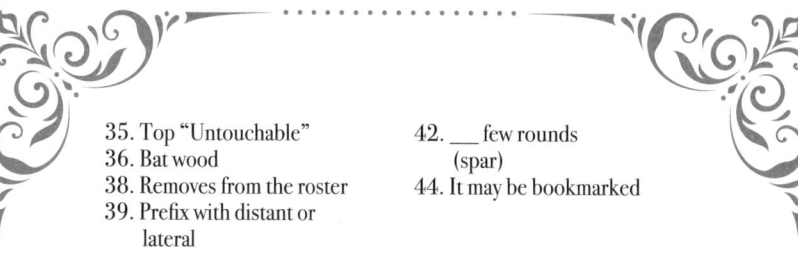

Answers on page 109.

Pop Quiz

In the first *Home Alone* movie, where does the McCallister family go to spend Christmas?

A. New York City, New York
B. Chicago, Illinois
C. Paris, France
D. Miami, Florida

Answer on page 109.

Meet Me Under the Mistletoe

Cryptograms are messages in substitution code. Break the code to read the message. For example, THE SMART CAT might become FVO QWGDF JGF if F is substituted for T, V for H, O for E, and so on.

GYNUZSUOS XZPEUN PDS LOQEB PZGONU

SKSDJCHSDS PEB PRUQPZZJ LYDNU ADSC

YE UHS UDOXYRN.

Answer on page 109.

Star Power

Fill each of the squares in the grid so that every green star is surrounded by a digit from 1 to 8 with no repeats.

Answers on page 109.

P Is for Poinsettia

PAJAMAS
PARADE
PARTRIDGE
PARTY
PASTRIES
PEACE
PECAN PIE
PEPPERMINT
PHOTOGRAPH
PIANO
PINECONE

PIPERS PIPING
PLAID
PLENTIFUL
POINSETTIA
POLAR
POPCORN STRING
POSTCARD
PRANCER
PRESENTS
PUDDING
PUNCH

```
O A L P A G M Y Q H C N U P B S
V Z E I X D I M S K S N X R U F
M P P X C R K P O S T C A R D G
H E O K A P O I N S E T T I A N
P P L P A R A D E F R L B P N I
A P A A A U O N A I P S M E W P
R E R R G J G X E A A W J A R I
G R E T N P A S T R I E S C L P
O M N R I Y T M W A S J F E Y S
T I O I D W L F A L R H G R V R
O N C D D N F R R S K I V U L E
H T E G U P G S T N E S E R P P
P P N E P B O D I A L P F M G I
H V I V P Y U E I P N A C E P P
H I P P O P C O R N S T R I N G
P R A N C E R L U F I T N E L P
```

Answers on page 110.

Under the Tree

Change just one letter on each line to go from the top word to the bottom word. Do not change the order of the letters. You must have a common English word at each step.

GIFT

___

___

___

PILE

Answers on page 110.

Say What?

Below is a group of words that, when properly arranged in the blanks, reveal a quote from Dale Evans.

time   action   Christmas   we   is   time

"Christmas _____ love in _____. Every _____ _____ love, every _____ we give, it's _____."

Answers on page 110.

Kris Kringle

Using the following list of clues, find words of four or five letters hidden in the phrase KRIS KRINGLE.

1. Minor miss _____
2. Fine fabric _____
3. Oblong coil of yarn _____
4. Compare _____
5. Wash off _____
6. Where you may do answer 5 _____
7. Horse directors _____
8. Spooky lake? _____
9. Period of rule _____
10. Gifts on the fifth day of Christmas _____
11. Small, slender lizard _____
12. Skate place _____

Answers on page 110.

Skating Rink

ACROSS
1. Winter Olympics event
12. "It ___" (reply to "Who's there?")
13. Seltzer opener
14. Camelot lady
15. Hardly a seagoer
17. Tolkien tree creatures
18. Look for
19. Tornado-riding terrier
21. Type of bridge
24. Specify
27. Expose to oxygen
28. Bullfighting yell
29. Bingo cousin
31. How-___ (guides)
32. "You bet!"
34. Small coin
35. Werner ___ , inventor of loop jump in 1-Across
37. United ___ Emirates
38. Punch bowl item
42. Cyborg prefix
44. "Million Dollar Baby" director
47. Shore scavenger
48. "Now I get it!"
49. Stressful suffix for press
50. Teardrop shape twirl on ice

DOWN
1. Nike competitor
2. Eyewitness's phrase
3. Gershon of film
4. Jamaican figure
5. Horror film street
6. Reggae relative
7. ___ ethics developed by Immanuel
8. Risk falling
9. Begin something new
10. Tiny criticism
11. Dept. store inventory
16. Cubes with spots
20. Bread spread
22. School for princes
23. Chill out
24. Film ___ (movie genre)
25. "For ___ know..."
26. Fusible
29. Cake with raisins
30. Glance
33. Promenade
34. Gullet
36. John of pop music
39. Decorate
40. "Footloose" singer
41. Early paradise
42. Primary colors of light: abbr.
43. French agreement
45. "I knew it!"
46. Nine-digit ID

Matching

Match each holiday greeting to the language it comes from.

1. Joyeux Noël
2. Frohe Weihnachten
3. Wesołych Świąt
4. Veselé Vánoce

A. Czech
B. German
C. French
D. Polish

Answers on page 111.

Chr_stm_s D_nn_r

Below is a list of traditional Christmas dishes, but they lost the vowels A, E, I, O, and U, as well as any punctuation and spaces between words. Can you figure out the missing vowels and name each item in the list below?

1. HNYGLZDHM
2. MNCMTP
3. WLDRFSLD
4. MSHDPTTS
5. RSTDCRRTS
6. CRNBRRYSC
7. DVLDGGS
8. BFWLLNGTN

Answers on page 111.

Star Power

Fill each of the squares in the grid so that every green star is surrounded by a digit from 1 to 8 with no repeats.

Answers on page 111.

Christmas Movies

A CHARLIE BROWN (Christmas)
(A) CHRISTMAS STORY
ELF
FROSTY (the Snowman)
FROZEN
(The) HOLIDAY
HOME ALONE
HOW THE GRINCH (Stole Christmas)
JINGLE JANGLE: (A Christmas Journey)
KLAUS
LOVE ACTUALLY
MIRACLE (on 34th Street)
(The) NIGHTMARE BEFORE (Christmas)
(The) POLAR EXPRESS
(The) SANTA CLAUS
(It's a) WONDERFUL LIFE

```
E O Q Q Q F C P K L A U S M E L
N S S E R P X E R A L O P R G F
O E F I L L U F R E D N O W G F
L K P G M T V V N Q F F B B F R
A P V Z N I I A G R E I C L Q O
E L J A A M C Y N B P A E H E S
M N H C N I R G E H T W O H C T
O J G E I G R R J I B A C M R Y
H U Y A C H A R L I E B R O W N
S N F P J M O A F N E Z O R F U
I Z Q C T Z Y A D I L O H O V O
Y E C H R I S T M A S S T O R Y
W B G F O U C Q O M I R A C L E
T I C Y L L A U T C A E V O L A
N Y J S A N T A C L A U S G D U
P Y E L G N A J E L G N I J H W
```

Answers on page 112.

Ignominious Christmas Gift

Change just one letter on each line to go from the top word to the bottom word. Do not change the order of the letters. You must have a common English word at each step.

COAL

_____

_____

_____

_____   old-fashioned livestock call

SOCK

Answers on page 112.

Either/Or

Complete the sentence with two words that are anagrams of each other (e.g. CARE and RACE).

She cut a slice out of the _____ of _____ pudding served for dessert.

Answers on page 112.

Picture This

Place each of the 15 boxes in the 3 by 5 grid below so that they form a holiday picture. Do this without cutting the page apart: Use only your eyes.

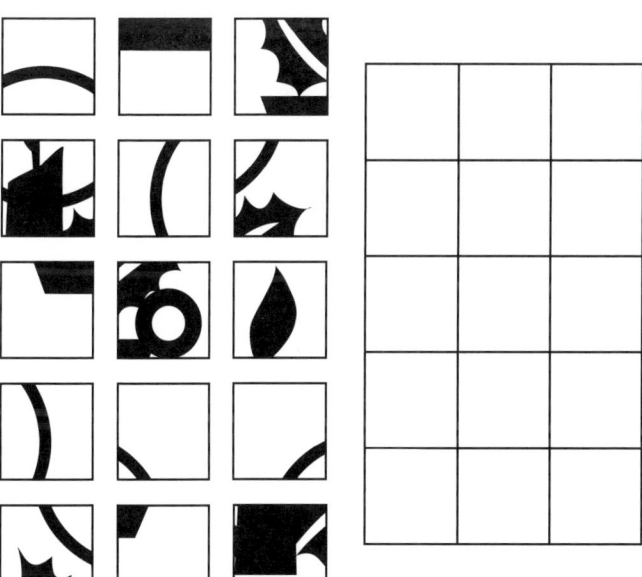

Answer on page 112.

Winter Flying Sport

ACROSS
1. U.F.C. fighting style
4. Highest point
8. Alone
12. Plastic device
13. Thin cut
14. Organic compound
15. Norm: abbr.
16. ZZ Top song
17. Red shade
18. Ski jump referee points: 2 wds.
21. Craft
22. ___ Francisco
23. Under the influence
26. Nuclear physics Nobelist, Enrico ___
29. Method for increasing the web traffic: abbr.
30. Informer
32. Five-rings logo org.
33. Limestone formation
36. Nigerian language
39. Hasten
41. Photog's item: abbr.
42. Arrival zone for Matti Nykanen, e.g.: 2 wds.
47. No longer mint
49. Flair
50. ER notation
51. Wizard, old-style
52. Large prefix
53. 12, to 4 and 6: math abbr.
54. Trudge
55. Figure-skating jump
56. Age-determining stat

DOWN
1. Fail to see
2. Mixed breed
3. GPS input, slangily
4. To the rear
5. Grouping
6. Catchall category: abbr.
7. Cultural spirit
8. Peaceful
9. Burden
10. High tennis shot
11. ___ Games
19. Chinese philosopher, ___-tzu
20. UK fliers: abbr.
23. Mermaid's home
24. Rocky pinnacle
25. Dawn to dusk
27. Chest bone
28. Extinct bird of New Zealand
29. One of the winter sports: 2 wds.
31. Cargo capacity
34. Out of the sun
35. Pewter component
37. Monarch-related

38. "That's awful!"
40. Swelling
42. Toy block brand
43. Holm oak
44. Without purpose
45. Bonkers
46. Young sheep
48. Baseball's Bando

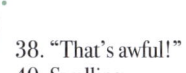

Pop Quiz

The first artificial Christmas trees were made in Germany.

____ True   ____ False

Answer on page 113.

The Meaning of Eggnog

Cryptograms are messages in substitution code. Break the code to read the message. For example, THE SMART CAT might become FVO QWGDF JGF if F is substituted for T, V for H, O for E, and so on.

KCR LTJB "RAAPTA" WP TNB RPANWYC

NWKRJONNI XROPY "RAA WP O NWKKNR SEG."

Answer on page 113.

Star Power

Fill each of the squares in the grid so that every green star is surrounded by a digit from 1 to 8 with no repeats.

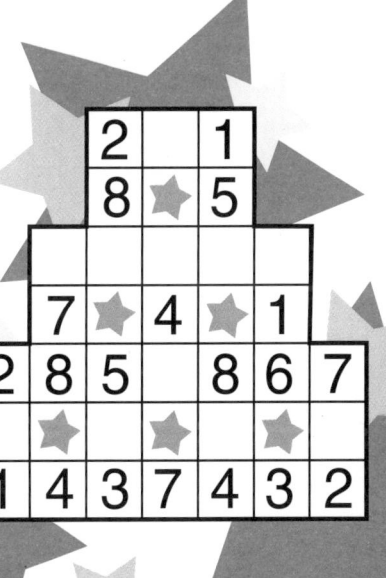

Answers on page 113.

Christmas Songs

BABY, IT'S COLD (Outside)
DECK (the) HALLS
FELIZ NAVIDAD
(Up on the) HOUSETOP
I'LL BE HOME (for Christmas)
JINGLE (Bells)
LET IT SNOW
LINUS (and) LUCY
MISTLETOE
O TANNENBAUM
SANTA TELL ME
SILENT NIGHT
SILVER BELLS
SLEIGH RIDE
(Christmas) TREE FARM
WONDERFUL (Christmastime)

```
F Y T P W A D W I C P P S T N S
E E H G W L T V N F O L A I X U
L M G V X I Z B C T L G N M Z Q
I O I Z H A L W E E J T T J L U
Z H N Q K W Q S B R I R A H X Z
N E T Q K Q U R A O N E T D C O
A B N N D O E P B K G E E E M T
V L E I H V L G Y O L F L C I A
I L L D L Y G E I Q E A L K S N
D I I I F G B R T B R R M H T N
A Y S Z C T R F S I K M E A L E
D L I N U S L U C Y T R G L E N
N L U F R E D N O W I S Y L T B
C P M G Y N G G L A S F N S O A
U D K L K K V X D V I G H O E U
G I E D I R H G I E L S E Y W M
```

Answers on page 114.

The Spirit of Christmas

Change just one letter on each line to go from the top word to the bottom word. Do not change the order of the letters. You must have a common English word at each step.

HOPE

____

____

____

____

WISH

Answers on page 114.

Say What?

Below is a group of words that, when properly arranged in the blanks, reveal a quote from Charles Schulz.

something   someone   doing   little

"Christmas is _____ a _____ _____ extra for _____."

Answers on page 114.

Joy to the World

Using the following list of clues, find words of four or five letters hidden in the phrase
JOY TO THE WORLD.

1. Some sweatshirts have one _____
2. Proceed briskly _____
3. Dog's cry _____
4. Cat's cry _____
5. Put on a party _____
6. Sheep's undercoat _____
7. Penned _____
8. Spoke _____
9. Goes under a pillow _____
10. Ancient handheld harp _____
11. Wharf _____
12. Payment given in some marriages _____

Answers on page 114.

Spotlight on St. Nick

ACROSS
1. Garland and Dench
6. Umps' cohorts
10. This-and-that dish
14. A point ahead
15. Scat singer Fitzgerald
16. First-class
17. St. Nick's cargo
19. Cereal grasses
20. Govt. ecological watchdog group
21. Electric light
22. Stitched connection
24. Pigpen
25. ___ Paulo, Brazil
26. Formal headwear
29. St. Nick's place of business
31. New Zealand parrot
32. Contributors
35. Wordplay experts
37. Melville's "Typee" sequel
38. Carry with difficulty
39. Eye part
40. Landscaper
43. Formal, informally
45. A-Team member
46. St. Nick's team
48. Compounds of gurus
50. Tidal outflow
51. Multiply-curved wheel
54. Sit
55. With regard to
56. SHO rival
57. Winter white
59. A.k.a. St. Nick
62. Fireside yarn
63. Ancient Peruvian
64. Thicket of trees
65. Washstand pitcher
66. Satiric comic Mort
67. Donkeys

DOWN
1. Ferrer and Canseco
2. Inappropriate
3. Rot
4. Really big laugh
5. Promoter
6. Captured back
7. North Carolina university
8. Soar
9. Poet Siegfried
10. Songstress McLachlan
11. St. Nick's elves
12. Opposite of WSW
13. Unseld or Craven
18. Dreads
23. Omar of "House"
26. Hired muscle
27. Hatcher and Garr
28. Smart-alecky
29. Potbelly fuel
30. Reject with distain

32. Religious tenet
33. Sharif and Bradley
34. St. Nick's whereabouts
36. Amphitheater level
38. Luau souvenirs
41. Notable periods
42. Goddess of vengeance
43. "Leap of Faith" star Winger
44. Daphne Du Maurier novel
47. Of the teeth

49. Oarsman
51. Cowboy leggings
52. Ill-treatment
53. Israelites' leader
55. $\frac{1}{36}$ of a yard
57. Sault ___ Marie
58. Slangy turndown
60. Gasteyer of "Mean Girls"
61. ___ Angeles

Pop Quiz

Which traditional song came first, "Jingle Bells" or "Up on a Housetop"?

Answer on page 115.

Jolabokaflod

Cryptograms are messages in substitution code. Break the code to read the message. For example, THE SMART CAT might become FVO QWGDF JGF if F is substituted for T, V for H, O for E, and so on.

HGO JHJSDIP WMODINWM RPINWRWHG

WGUHDUOQ OXMEIGLWGL GOV AHHCQ

VWRE TIFWDY FOFAOPQ IGN POINWGL REOF

HG MEPWQRFIQ OUO. REO RPINWRWHG VIQ

JHJSDIPWZON NSPWGL REO QOMHGN VHPDN VIP,

VEOG JIJOP VIQ HGO HT REO TOV REWGLQ GHR

PIRWHGON WG WMODIGN.

Answer on page 115.

Star Power

Fill each of the squares in the grid so that every green star is surrounded by a digit from 1 to 8 with no repeats.

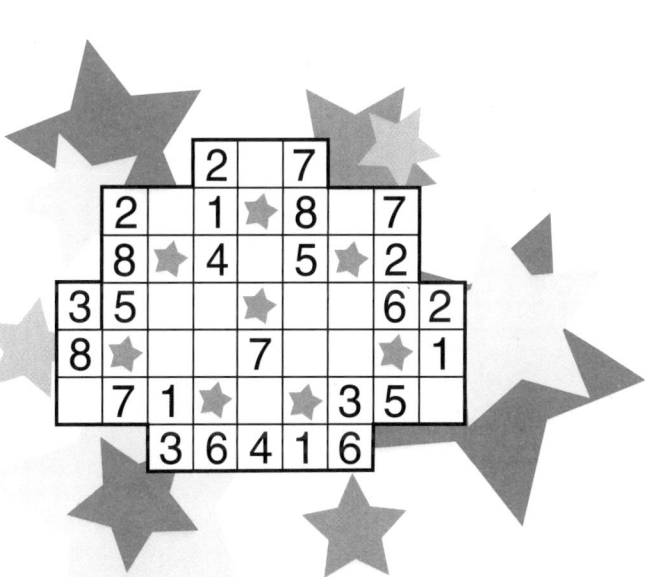

Answers on page 115.

F Is for Figgy Pudding

FABULOUS	FLANNEL
FAMILY	FLURRIES
FANCY	FOLKLORE
FANTASTIC	FREEZING
FAWN	FRENCH HENS
FEAST	FRESH SNOW
FESTIVAL	FRIENDS
FIGGY PUDDING	FROLIC
FILMS	FRUITCAKE
FIR TREE	FUDGE
FIREPLACE	FUZZY

```
E N S F Z E I G S S M L I F V L
R Z Y J R K E K A C T I U R F T
O B E K J E F R I E N D S N I R
L F G L T H S N E H H C N E R F
K I D D C V C H K A I U H Y E I
L R U C P C I T S A T N A F P G
O T F F R E E Z I N G L K C L G
F R Z H U F O K E R O F F H A Y
L E A S I O A J B A R W Y S C P
E E Q K L V X B R U A Q E V E U
N O C I L O R F U H Y I N F L D
N U F E S T I V A L R H T A F D
A V J I F E A S T R O W L W A I
L F A M I L Y M U Q G U L N N N
F M M N U U S L O U C N S P C G
F U Z Z Y N F J F W C Y U M Y M
```

Answers on page 116.

Dress the Tree

Change just one letter on each line to go from the top word to the bottom word. Do not change the order of the letters. You must have a common English word at each step.

TRIM

_____

_____

_____ leave it

_____

CROP

Answers on page 116.

Either/Or

Complete the sentence with two words that are anagrams of each other (e.g. CARE and RACE).

Add a personal ____ to Christmas cards to share gratitude and capture the thoughtful ____ of the season.

Answers on page 116.

Snowflake

Using the following list of clues, find words of four or five letters hidden in the phrase
SNOWFLAKE.

1. Christmas or a song _____
2. Flattering deer? _____
3. Hunk of bread _____
4. Pedestrian's sign _____
5. Lounging spot _____
6. Option on a test _____
7. Ballet bird _____
8. Added to a table when hosting family _____
9. Eat like an animal _____
10. 1990 Movie *Home* _____
11. Wax for an envelope _____
12. Skin care ingredient _____

Answers on page 116.

Secret Santa

ACROSS
1. Arnold has big ones
5. Net auction site
9. Act melodramatically
14. Urban eyesore
15. Fizzy drink
16. Deep sleep
17. Seasonal buyers
20. Clap hands
21. Disputed part of Ecuador east of the Andes
22. Results of a flogging
23. Skye of "Say Anything"
24. Homer king Hank
27. Houdini feat
32. What there are two of in this puzzle's long answers
35. "Totally cool!"
37. Start of many a hymn
38. Be in prosperous circumstances
42. Ticket part
43. "In ___" (Nirvana album)
44. Pub brew
45. Cyberspace V.I.P.'s
48. Hawaiian crow
50. List wrapup
52. Board at an inn
56. Like Cyclops
60. Without end
62. 1954 Dr. Seuss book
64. Signal, as to an auctioneer
65. Palindromic comics dog
66. It's heard from one taking off
67. Speak at length
68. James of "The Godfather"
69. Role for Julia

DOWN
1. "Poppycock!"
2. Take the honey and run
3. Mea ___
4. Danish novelist Peter Hoeg's title character
5. Seesaw sitter in verse
6. Hopalong Cassidy's last name
7. TV plugs
8. Popular Internet portal
9. Catches sight of
10. Sulk
11. Sign on a store door
12. Civil wrong
13. Limerick language
18. Coca-Cola brand name
19. Novelist Sarah ___ Jewett
23. All told
25. Avg. size
26. Diamond Head locale
28. Runner Sebastian
29. Turkish bigwig
30. Crawl space?
31. One of a cube's dozen

32. Oil company with a toy truck line
33. Like some high-fiber cereal
34. Actors Erwin and Gilliam
36. 1977 Scott Turow book
39. "Oz" broadcaster
40. Singer's syllable
41. Katie or Sherlock
46. Cactus drug
47. Light machine gun
49. Put bubbles in
51. For a special purpose
53. Egypt's Sadat
54. Christine of "Swing Shift"
55. "McSorley's Bar" painter
56. "Not that!"
57. Koh-i-___ diamond
58. "Das Rheingold" goddess
59. State, to a Quebecer
60. "I could ___ horse!"
61. Disney film of 1982 that was also a video game
63. Zeta's follower

Answers on page 116.

Miles and Miles of Christmas Cheer

Cryptograms are messages in substitution code. Break the code to read the message. For example, THE SMART CAT might become FVO QWGDF JGF if F is substituted for T, V for H, O for E, and so on.

RHEYAPX QKNN DPKFM YG LHKUPEEYM, HKNTHG,

YM HGN HD QRN EPKTNMQ LRKYMQFPM QKNN

DPKFM YG QRN VHKEA. HG PUKPTN, QRNX MRYI

HSQ POHSQ P FYEEYHG QKNNM INK XNPK.

Answer on page 117.

Matching

Match each item to its corresponding number in "The Twelve Days of Christmas."

1. Pipers Piping   A. 4
2. Partridge in a Pear Tree   B. 11
3. Calling Birds   C. 1
4. Ladies Dancing   D. 9

Answers on page 117.

Pop Quiz

The Christmas standard popularized by Bing Crosby, "I'll Be Home for Christmas," was originally published in this year.

A. 1917
B. 1918
C. 1941
D. 1943

Answer on page 117.

Merry and BRIGHT

Cryptograms are messages in substitution code. Break the code to read the message. For example, THE SMART CAT might become FVO QWGDF JGF if F is substituted for T, V for H, O for E, and so on.

SDW BKILTQ PLAGWBWHHWP ADPEQSIKQ

SPWW EJ JWV YLPG AESY EQ HES VESD LUWP

BEBSY SDLTQKJO HWO HECDSQ, VDEAD EQ

LUWP BEUW IEHWQ LB VEPW.

Answer on page 117.

Gifts Handmade with Love

ARTWORK	MUG
BATH BOMB	ORNAMENT
BLANKET	PHOTO ALBUM
BODY SCRUB	POT HOLDER
BOOKMARK	POTTERY
CANDLE	PRESERVES
COOKIES	QUILT
DREAM CATCHER	SCARF
EMBROIDERY	SOAP
JEWELRY	STUFFED ANIMAL
LOTION	WOODEN SPOON

```
H R V S W O O D E N S P O O N K
M E R R Y F V L O T I O N H I R
S D R E H C T A C M A E R D A O
T L M M B I R X Y R E T T O P W
U O U S Z B A T H B O M B H S T
Y H B E R L O L P J O I Z K N R
R T L V Q A M D Q U I L T R I A
E O A R I N U U Y W X N P A Z V
D P O E T K G F Z S E L A M P G
I W T S F E K Y H M C J O K F S
O H O E X T R Y A Q A R S O S E
R M H R Y L O N Z Y N Q U O C I
B Y P P E L R W Z T D J P B A K
M O P W H O N G R U L S U O R O
E J E I U B D V C W E E B A F O
X J L A M I N A D E F F U T S C
```

Answers on page 117.

Star Power

Fill each of the squares in the grid so that every green star is surrounded by a digit from 1 to 8 with no repeats.

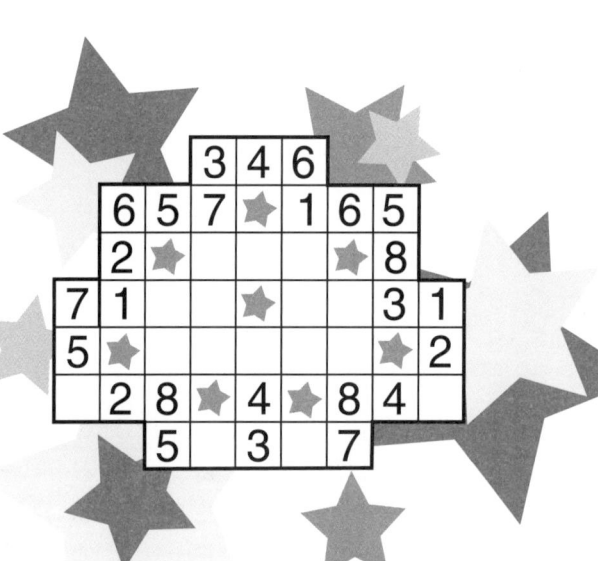

Answers on page 118.

A Holiday Hoard!

Change just one letter on each line to go from the top word to the bottom word. Do not change the order of the letters. You must have a common English word at each step.

GIFT

_____

_____

_____   get digging

_____

PILE

Answers on page 118.

Either / Or

Complete the sentence with two words that are anagrams of each other (e.g. CARE and RACE).

Braving the chilly wind from the _____, all the shoppers were bundled in their _____ to visit the Christmas market.

Answers on page 118.

Hiding Some Christmas Things

ACROSS
1. Kismet
5. Army chow
9. Plays and such
14. Norwegian king
15. Southernmost Great Lake
16. External
17. Tennis ace Sampras
18. Clay deposit
19. Hot ___ buns
20. Christmas character disguised as a jazz guitarist?
23. "An Inconvenient Truth" narrator
24. Big web portal
25. Wine from Jerez
28. It dissolved in 1991: abbr.
30. "Pow!"
33. Went sniggling
34. On the ocean
35. Some arias
36. Christmas plant hiding in a showbiz TV show?
39. Make more watery
40. "Don't Hassel the ___": "Baywatch" star motto
41. Curses
42. Twenty-volume dictionary: abbr.
43. Informal greeting
44. Big-brimmed bonnet
45. Flattens, for short
46. Kind of music or medicine
47. Christmas song hiding in a southeastern state?
53. Portuguese enclave in China
54. "It's beginning to look ___ like..."
55. Smooth sailing
57. Hawke of "Dead Poets Society"
58. Ritzy
59. Tizzy
60. "A Confederacy of Dunces" author
61. Head of France?
62. Garden hopper

DOWN
1. Dandy
2. A Baldwin
3. Soho sign-off
4. Christmas tree type
5. Down ___ lane
6. Obliterate
7. Galahad and others
8. Actress Ward
9. Advanced degree holder
10. Cracker-barrel
11. Gobs
12. Western elevation
13. Word in the MGM motto
21. Byron and Tennyson, e.g.
22. Like many French vowels
25. Defense group abolished in 1977: abbr.

26. Anne of "Men in Trees"
27. Spanish hero of yore
28. "The good ol' ___"
29. Egotist's obsession
30. Diner seat
31. Hilo hello
32. Central part
34. Mate's shout
35. Most elegant
37. "Skewer" in Istanbul
38. "Try it, ___ like it!"
43. Knee-slapper

44. Comfort
45. African cattle pen
46. "The Road Not Taken" poet
47. Kosovo force
48. Eight in Ecuador
49. Rank above 1st Lt.: abbr.
50. Soothing botanical
51. Prefix with second
52. Where Bhutan is
53. Bumped into
56. Airport abbr.

Answers on page 118.

Drummer Boy

Using the following list of clues, find words of four or five letters hidden in the phrase
DRUMMER BOY.

1. After shower attire _____
2. Corpus _____
3. Full of ennui _____
4. Christmas cheer _____
5. Command _____
6. Follow answer 5 _____
7. Forest fruit _____
8. Spirited card game? _____
9. Early song cut _____
10. Sullen _____
11. July's birthstone _____
12. "A little bird told me..." _____

Answers on page 118.

Matching

Match each item to its corresponding number in "The Twelve Days of Christmas."

1. Geese A-Laying
2. Maids A-Milking
3. French Hens
4. Drummers Drumming

A. 12
B. 8
C. 6
D. 3

Answers on page 119.

M_d_rn S_ng_rs

Below is a list of contemporary Christmas music singers, but they lost the vowels A, E, I, O, and U, as well as any punctuation and spaces between words. Can you figure out the missing vowels and name each artist in the list below?

1. KCYMSGRVS
2. MRHCRY
3. JSTNBBR
4. RNGRND
5. SFJNSTVNS
6. KLLYCLRKSN
7. MCHLBBL
8. CRLYRJPSN

Answers on page 119.

On the Nice List

ACCOUNTABLE	INTEGRITY
CAREFUL	KIND
COMPASSIONATE	LOYAL
DILIGENT	OPTIMISTIC
EMPATHETIC	PATIENT
FAIR	RESPONSIBLE
GENEROUS	SELFLESS
GIVING	SUPPORTIVE
GRATEFUL	THOUGHTFUL
HONEST	UNDERSTANDING
HUMBLE	WISE

```
C M O H G C F I S C A R E F U L
K J G F N Z A Z I D X K C B S R
L Z Y I I B I G H T N E I T A P
N M T T D H R D I L I G E N T E
C S F J N E V I T R O P P U S Y
C O M P A S S I O N A T E F J T
C S U N T C G I V I N G L F C I
I E D D S J C E L B M U H G I R
T L N H R E A O O S F X T R T G
S F I O E T R R U T C D P A E E
I L K N D Q N O H N R Z L T H T
M E M E N Y R G T Q T A A E T N
I S R S U E U E S I W A D F A I
T S H T N O E L O Y A L B U P J
P W Z E H K H M H C L V P L M H
O E G T H E L B I S N O P S E R
```

Answers on page 119.

Star Power

Fill each of the squares in the grid so that every green star is surrounded by a digit from 1 to 8 with no repeats.

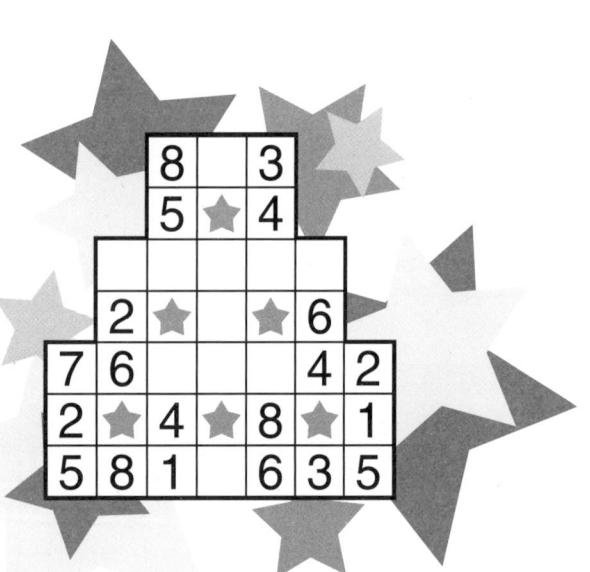

Answers on page 119.

Winter Fun

Change just one letter on each line to go from the top word to the bottom word. Do not change the order of the letters. You must have a common English word at each step.

SNOW

_____

_____

_____ boat

_____

SKIS

Answers on page 120.

Either / Or

Complete the sentence with two words that are anagrams of each other (e.g. CARE and RACE).

On the _____ winter evening, the Christmas tree glittered with strips of sparkling _____.

Answers on page 120.

Christmas at the Movies

ACROSS
1. Peck, for one
5. Humpback herds
9. Gives off coherent light
14. Dutch treat
15. Others, to Octavian
16. Taper off
17. Philosopher Descartes
18. Skip a turn
19. Dr. Seuss's "___ Only Old Once!"
20. 1970 film based on an Edith Nesbit novel, with "The"
23. Talese's "Honor ___ Father"
24. Generic John
25. Ring surface
28. Have a fowl diet?
32. Grave letters
35. Bring a smile to
37. Drops from the sky
38. Zola heroine
39. 1996 movie with Arnold Schwarzenegger
42. Sleep ___ (decide tomorrow)
43. Not taped
44. What's happening
45. "Arabian Nights" menace
46. Actress Hudgens of "High School Musical 2"
48. Prepare to drag
49. Used a stool
50. Had a little lamb
52. 1987 Yuletide classic starring Keshia Knight Pulliam, with "The"
61. Battlezone maker
62. Michelle of "Crouching Tiger, Hidden Dragon"
63. Track event
64. Wee bits
65. Branch headquarters?
66. The real Popeye Doyle
67. Hang around
68. Emcee
69. Deep-six

DOWN
1. "Galloping Gourmet" Graham
2. Sneaking suspicion
3. ___-Flush
4. Silvery food fish
5. Fruit with a musky tang
6. Oil of ___
7. Music buy
8. Robe closer
9. Hide
10. Dwelling
11. Dino's tail?
12. French 101 verb
13. No longer hidden

21. Potter's need
22. "___ know" ("Beats me")
25. Big-time
26. Essential acid
27. Costume for "I, Claudius"
29. Get into condition
30. Break off, in glacier country
31. Annoys
32. Less cooked
33. Like some chatter
34. Premium channel
36. Bilko, e.g.
38. Ariz. neighbor
40. Gladden
41. Ledger of "A Knight's Tale"
46. Overnight bag
47. Fragrant packet
49. Watchband
51. Everglades wader
52. ___-back (relaxed)
53. "Believe ___ not"
54. Breezy sendoff
55. Old story
56. Sleek, in car lingo
57. Low digits
58. Othello's treacherous ensign
59. Some VCRs
60. Camera part

Answers on page 120.

Picture This

Place each of the 16 boxes in the 4 by 4 grid below so that they form a jingling holiday picture. Do this without cutting the page apart: Use only your eyes.

Answer on page 120.

Pop Quiz

The song "Silver Bells" originally went by this title:

A. "Jingling Bells"
B. "Tinkle Bells"
C. "Pretty Bells"
D. "Silver Chimes"

Answer on page 120.

Kalle Anka

Cryptograms are messages in substitution code. Break the code to read the message. For example, THE SMART CAT might become FVO QWGDF JGF if F is substituted for T, V for H, O for E, and so on.

DC NHMSPQBJP LTL SC PULGLC, JYBDPQ HJYE

QHL NDRCQMX PSQP GDUC JQ QHMLL SC QHL

JEQLMCDDC QD UJQNH J GDCJYG GRNA NHMSPQBJP

PFLNSJY QHJQ JSMP LTLMX XLJM.

Answer on page 121.

N Is for Noel

NATIVITY
NATURE
NAUGHTY
NAVIGATE
NEATLY WRAPPED
NECTARINE
NEEDLEWORK
NEIGHBORS
NEST
NEW YEAR
NICE

NIGHTCAP
NIPPING
NOBLE
NORDIC
NORTH POLE
NOSTALGIA
NOURISHMENT
NOVELTY
NUMB
NURTURE
NUZZLING

```
V Q N A L N E N Y N U R T U R E
G R E E O A T E S J D D U T Y D
U U S Y S T A W R Y Z E E H Z U
A E T T G I G Y Y W Q P R V U X
N G K L N V I E W G Q P U V P N
E N R E I I V A X M E A T D N A
I O O V P T A R T L A R A L P U
G B W O P Y N E O X I W N N A G
H L E N I O C P I K G Y O U C H
B E L A N I H P M B L L R Z T T
O G D D N T Z H M L A T F Z H Y
R S E U R C M U D K T A Y L G D
S K E O M O N O V S S E H I I C
T T N E M H S I R U O N F N N Y
A D A V N O R D I C N T M G N S
Z Q C Q K N R E N I R A T C E N
```

Answers on page 121.

Star Power

Fill each of the squares in the grid so that every green star is surrounded by a digit from 1 to 8 with no repeats.

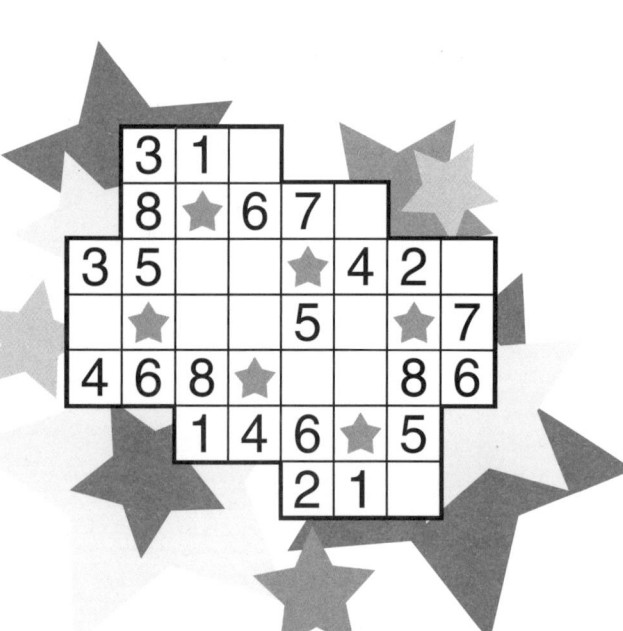

Answers on page 121.

Sleigh Bells Ring

Change just one letter on each line to go from the top word to the bottom word. Do not change the order of the letters. You must have a common English word at each step.

BELL

_____

_____

_____

_____

_____

RING

Answers on page 121.

Say What?

Below is a group of words that, when properly arranged in the blanks, reveal a quote from Roy L. Smith.

under not heart who Christmas tree find

He _____ has _____ _____ in his _____ will never _____ it _____ a _____.

Answers on page 122.

Christmas Tunes

ACROSS
1. Chic and cool
5. Move like a cloud
9. Lion king
14. Punjabi princess
15. TV, slangily, with "the"
16. Dotcom casualty of March 7, 2001
17. Ballpark figures: abbr.
18. Wields
19. "Buffalo Stance" singer Cherry
20. 1940 Irving Berlin song
23. Like a doily
24. Parts of a day: abbr.
25. "This way"
28. Met solo
30. 1989 play about Capote
33. Get together
34. Lyricist ___ Jay Lerner
35. Unfavorable picnic forecast
36. 1916 song by a Ukrainian composer
39. Hamburg's river
40. Colorado Indians
41. Draw forth
42. Canny
43. Ivan the Terrible, for one
44. Closer to 50-50
45. Sailor's yes
46. Fencers' match
47. Song first released by Bobby Helms in 1957
54. "The Thinker" sculptor
55. ___-Rooter
56. "The heat ___"
57. Former Attorney General Edwin
58. "Walkabout" director Nicolas
59. Big fashion magazine
60. Wet wintry mix
61. Nimble
62. A portion

DOWN
1. Got bigger
2. Whip
3. Naysayer
4. Kissing come-on
5. Wire-and-plaster wall covering
6. Like an easy job
7. Prefix with mensch
8. Lucy's partner
9. Nissan compact
10. Entries on a list
11. Freeman of "Black Beauty"
12. To make informal farewells
13. Blond shade
21. Painting support
22. Stand out
25. Henry R. and Clare Boothe
26. Counting everything

27. Baseball Hall of Famer Puckett
28. Take in or let out
29. Cheerleaders' cries
30. Raptor's claw
31. Poet Rainer Maria ___
32. Al, Al Jr., or Bobby
34. Brut rival
35. Merrymaking activities
37. Small diving bird
38. Cut at an angle
43. Young swan
44. Funeral oration
45. Pernod flavoring
46. Discourage
47. "Piano Man" singer Billy
48. ___ fixe (obsessive thought)
49. Messes up
50. Betty of the bee-stung lips
51. Peace Prize city
52. Actor Meaney
53. Leg joint
54. Apt. units

Answers on page 122.

Mistletoe

Using the following list of clues, find words of five or six letters hidden in the word
MISTLETOE.

1. Overnight stop _____
2. Friendly face _____
3. A long, wide scarf _____
4. Word(s) on a spine _____
5. Squishy, sticky toy trend _____
6. Desirable cake description _____
7. Stamina _____
8. Folded breakfast _____
9. Dapple _____
10. Small sea key _____
11. Works hard _____
12. Ancestral emblem _____

Answers on page 122.

Matching

Match each classic Christmas song to its singer.

1. "A Holly Jolly Christmas"
2. "Santa Claus Is Coming to Town"
3. "Jingle Bell Rock"
4. "Feliz Navidad"

A. Bobby Helms
B. José Feliciano
C. Burl Ives
D. Harry Reser and His Band

Answers on page 122.

Th_ Cl_ss_cs

Below is a list of classic Christmas music singers, but they lost the vowels A, E, I, O, and U, as well as any punctuation and spaces between words. Can you figure out the missing vowels and name each artist in the list below?

1. NTKNGCL
2. DNMRTN
3. BNGCRSBY
4. BRLVS
5. LLFTZGRLD
6. DRLNLV
7. GNTRY
8. LSRMSTRNG

Answers on page 123.

Christmas Critters

CALF	PARTRIDGE
CARDINAL	PENGUIN
CARIBOU	POLAR BEAR
CHIPMUNK	PUPPY
ELK	RABBIT
FRENCH HEN	REINDEER
GOOSE	ROBIN
KITTEN	SWAN
LAMB	TURKEY
MOOSE	TURTLEDOVE
MOUSE	WHITETAIL DEER

```
S I K C N G O Y N L V P F F H I
J J T A R E E D N I E R W L P W
K N U M P I H C Z U T Q L A M B
G A Q C O U K L K B L Z J C P X
M J N A W S F C A R D I N A L U
X G E R B F B P E N G U I N R M
P J R I F K C V J E N D E W A Y
E K D B M R U A L N E T V N E Y
S I A O F O O X L I H U O F B E
U T P U X N O Y A B H R D G R F
O T Q K L E D S P O C K E K A W
M E L N Y Y H N E R N E L T L K
N N U P E S O O G U E Y T B O Y
H V P V Z E E G D I R T R A P I
N U U R A B B I T R F O U P J B
P A B R E E D L I A T E T I H W
```

Answers on page 123.

Star Power

Fill each of the squares in the grid so that every green star is surrounded by a digit from 1 to 8 with no repeats.

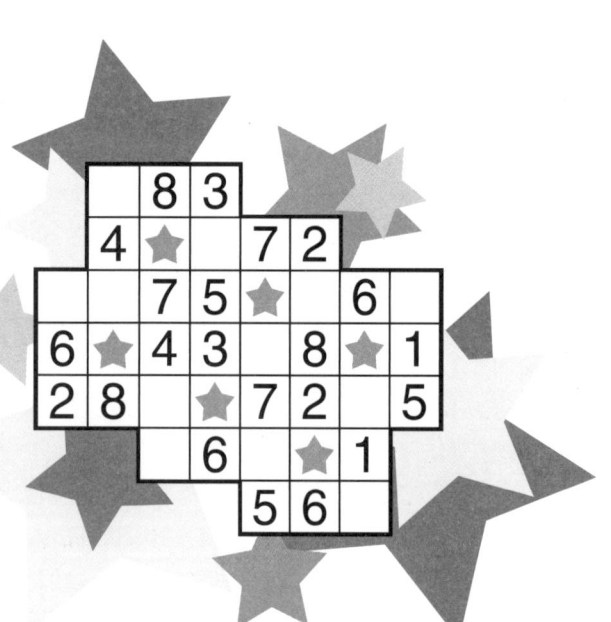

Answers on page 123.

Festive and Toasty

Change just one letter on each line to go from the top word to the bottom word. Do not change the order of the letters. You must have a common English word at each step.

YULE

____

____

____

____ cleans up

____

LOGS

Answers on page 123.

Either / Or

Complete the sentence with two words that are anagrams of each other (e.g. CARE and RACE).

The glow of the Christmas tree _____ sparkling ornaments and _____ neatly wrapped gifts.

Answers on page 123.

Deck the Halls

ACROSS
1. Wild swine
5. Starbucks order
10. Rice-A-___
14. Crucifix letters
15. Guardian spirit
16. "Think nothing ___!"
17. The first L in L.L. Bean
18. Manual transmission, informally
19. "There was an old lady who swallowed ___"
20. "Deck the halls with . . ."
23. Suffix with humor
24. Ages and ages
25. "Tell me something ___ know"
28. Rathskeller glass
30. Bearing
33. Old Mideast political union: abbr.
34. Samuel Pepys, for one
37. Government bureau
38. "Troll the ancient . . ."
41. Smidgen
42. Floral fruit rich in vitamin C
43. Coll. entrant's stat
44. Schooner support
45. Expressed disapproval
49. Conductor Zubin
51. MC's need, for short
53. Dutch piano center
54. "Strike the harp and . . ."
59. Poet Khayyam
61. In the know
62. Machu Picchu builder
63. Häagen-___
64. Singer Frankie
65. Tournament ranking
66. Pasta used in soups
67. Site of the Krupp steelworks
68. Word in a threat

DOWN
1. A hobbit and his namesakes
2. "Two to go" situation
3. Stir to action
4. Anchor part
5. Cow catcher
6. Playwright Chekhov
7. Happy weekend acronym
8. Word in many college names
9. City of northeast Nevada
10. "Charlie and the Chocolate Factory" author Dahl
11. "Time to leave"
12. Zilch
13. Theatrical suffix
21. Figure skater Sonja
22. Architect Maya
26. Scientist's sprinkle
27. Attempt
29. Between jobs
30. In the ___ of (surrounded by)
31. Shrink's remark
32. Leave one's mark?
35. Procter & Gamble razor brand

36. Jamaica's Ocho ___
37. Some bulbous sculptures
38. Cry of pain
39. Malone and Hornacek's team
40. Eighth letter, spelled out
41. Leo is its logo
44. Spring time in Paris
46. Bit of corn
47. Draws out
48. Noted libertine
50. Tailor's dummy, e.g.
51. Singer Haggard
52. Freeze closed, as some harbors
55. Cathedral area
56. "___ the night before..."
57. Dutch painter Franz ___
58. River from Ardennes to the Seine
59. Constable ___ ("Star Trek: Deep Space Nine")
60. Spoil

Answers on page 124.

Picture This

Place each of the 24 boxes in the 5 by 6 grid below so they form a picture of a beloved gift. Do this without cutting the page apart: Use only your eyes. Six boxes in the completed grid will remain blank.

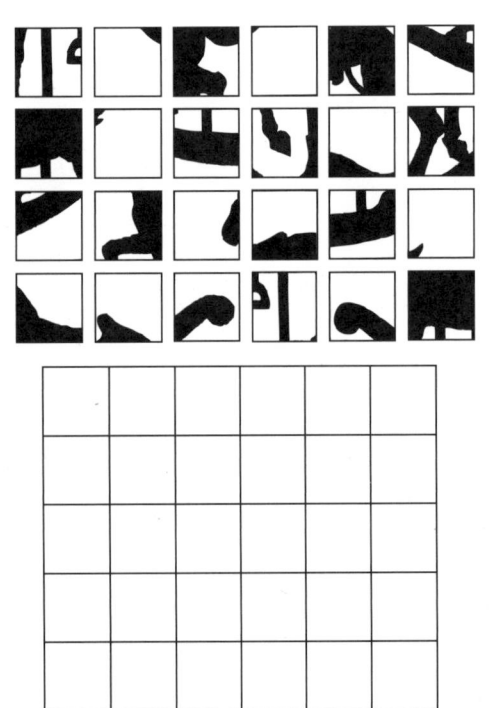

Answer on page 124.

Pop Quiz

Wassail, the drink offered to door-to-door carolers (wassailers) in England, is traditionally made from:

A. Mulled punch, often with oranges and apples
B. Cinnamon rum
C. Vodka
D. Root beer

Answer on page 124.

Sleigh Ride

Cryptograms are messages in substitution code. Break the code to read the message. For example, THE SMART CAT might become FVO QWGDF JGF if F is substituted for T, V for H, O for E, and so on.

QAY BGTHY KC OTJQT IFTSO CFXBJH ABO OFYBHA

VTO INYTQYP BJ QAY YTNFX JBJYQYYJQA IYJQSNX

RX VTOABJHQKJ BNUBJH–QAY OTGY TSQAKN VAK

PNYTGQ SL QAY AYTPFYOO AKNOYGTJ.

Answer on page 124.

Santa's Sleigh

BAG OF TOYS
CHIMNEY
CIRCLE THE GLOBE
COOKIES
FIREPLACE
FLIGHT
HEARTH
HOUSE
MAGIC
MILK
PEACE
REINDEER
ROOFTOP
RUDOLPH
SANTA CLAUS
SLEEPING KIDS
SLEIGH BELLS
SNOWFALL
SOOT
STARRY NIGHT
TRACKS
WISH LIST

```
T R Y B P B F X C H I M N E Y U
H U L P T A A I G T R A C K S J
G V A E H G D F R I H E M L E S
I G R A G O B P O E S B L B L U
L D E C I F G L C U P E O Q Q A
F H E E N T D T O J B L M C T L
S E D S Y O K H H H G X A O J C
F A N E R Y K X G E W G O C U A
P R I I R S Q I H X T S M N E T
O T E K A X E T P F M K Q W I N
T H R O T L E R T Y V U O N Q A
F M P O S L E E P I N G K I D S
O A D C C R W T T R U D O L P H
O G B R C O U Y Z U X K L I M N
R I I Z T R I S N O W F A L L J
N C N M T S I L H S I W A G R O
```

Answers on page 125.

Star Power

Fill each of the squares in the grid so that every green star is surrounded by a digit from 1 to 8 with no repeats.

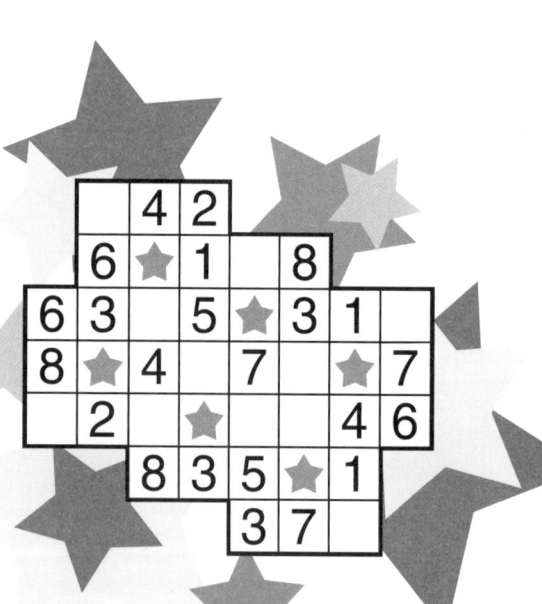

Answers on page 125.

Stay Warm

Change just one letter on each line to go from the top word to the bottom word. Do not change the order of the letters. You must have a common English word at each step.

COZY

_____

_____

_____   center of the Earth

_____

_____

FIRE

Answers on page 125.

Say What?

Below is a group of words that, when properly arranged in the blanks, reveal a quote from Bob Hope.

find glow great simplest Christmas we recall things happiness

When we _____ _____ past, _____ usually _____ that the _____ _____—not the _____ occasions—give off the greatest _____ of _____.

Answers on page 125.

Holiday Traditions

ACROSS
1. IV hooker-uppers
4. Location gizmo, for short
7. Latin music
12. Alley-___ (basketball maneuver)
13. Golden yrs. cache
14. Fairy tale character
15. Rowing tool
16. The opposite of "oui"
17. Swashbuckling Flynn
18. When we eat the big bird
21. Hearty swallow
22. Cherry or cranberry
23. When we give treats to children
26. Feel far from fine
29. Vein contents
30. Historic period
31. Isn't ungrammatical
32. Signaled "thumbs up"
33. When we party before Lent
35. Mr. Potato Head stick-on
36. Trickle through the cracks
37. When we give gifts to loved ones
42. Oversized
43. Poke fun at
44. Santa ___ winds
45. Newswoman Shriver
46. Blackjack necessity
47. Artist Maya
48. Oscar winner Marisa
49. Bosom buddy
50. Heart exam

DOWN
1. Cheer (for)
2. Genesis animal shelter
3. Spread out
4. Source of fan-shaped leaves
5. Old hands
6. Crooned a tune
7. Filmmaker Spielberg
8. Roll-on brand
9. Lonely, often coupled with "love"
10. Toil wearily
11. Best effort
19. Zeros
20. "___ you loud and clear"
23. Owl's cry
24. Becomes frayed
25. Make a blunder
26. Terrier type
27. Hysterical
28. Capt. saluters
31. Many a moon
33. Rum cocktail
34. Sanford of "The Jeffersons"
35. Bert's "Sesame Street" pal
37. "See you later"
38. Do damage to
39. Mouth, slangily

40. Flaky rock
41. Cristina ___ ("Grey's Anatomy" doctor)
42. UK clock setting

On the Naughty List

Using the following list of clues, find words of five or six letters hidden in the phrase NAUGHTY LIST.

1. Nick's honorific _____
2. Rudolph's nose descriptor _____
3. Material for a nightgown or tie _____
4. Colossus _____
5. Indicate _____
6. Not in the shade _____
7. A silent time _____
8. A plea _____
9. Hohoho is one _____
10. Comes from a star _____
11. May get you on the naughty list _____
12. Sailor's song _____

Answers on page 126.

Pop Quiz

The German title of "O Christmas Tree" is:

A. "O Tannabaum"
B. "O Tannebaum"
C. "O Tannenbaum"
D. "O Tanebbaum"

Answer on page 126.

New Popular Christmas Treat

Cryptograms are messages in substitution code. Break the code to read the message. For example, THE SMART CAT might become FVO QWGDF JGF if F is substituted for T, V for H, O for E, and so on.

TUDYGALQG TQSMYIG DPS AUI VQLPA BDZL

BPMVI AZ AQBBC QSM IKIDCAUYSV YS XIANIIS,

XPA JIJJIDLYSA XQDO UQG XITZLI Q BQKZDYAI

YS LZMIDS AYLIG.

Answer on page 126.

Santa and Company

AGIOS VASILIOS
BABBO NATALE
DED MOROZ
DER WEIHNACHTSMANN
DUN CHE LAO REN
FATHER CHRISTMAS
JOLLY OLD SAINT NICK
JOULUPUKKI
KRIS KRINGLE
NOEL BABA
PAPAI NOEL
PÈRE NÖEL
SAINT NICHOLAS
SAMICHLAUS
SANTA CLAUS
SINTERKLAAS

```
S S O D S A I N T N I C H O L A S
A G O T U E E L A T A N O B B A B
B J A I I N C S E W E L F C A O R
A T O A L G C Y U L U Z E L C D G
B L Q U Y I M H G A P U K V Z T D
L N F O L S S N E E L R D R M E I
E K T N S U I A R L E C R D D M Z
O O D I Y R P E V T A K A M S J Z
N Y Z H K Q N U N S B O O T S T E
J R G S J O S I K U O R R F N S T
Z D I P E T S J Q K O I Y E I A F
S R W L S R H I W Z I Y G L N W S
K L E O N I A P A P V X J A E X J
J O L L Y O L D S A I N T N I C K
R S A M T S I R H C R E H T A F X
S A M I C H L A U S A U H B L D Q
D E R W E I H N A C H T S M A N N
```

Answers on page 126.

Star Power

Fill each of the squares in the grid so that every green star is surrounded by a digit from 1 to 8 with no repeats.

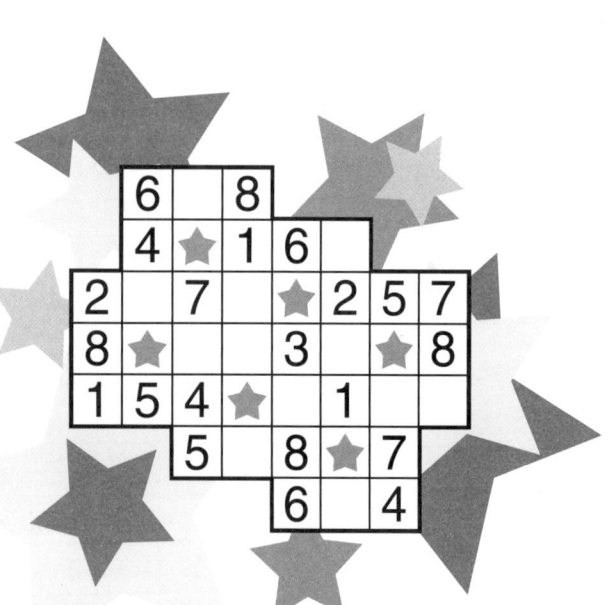

Answers on page 127.

Tree Topper

Change just one letter on each line to go from the top word to the bottom word. Do not change the order of the letters. You must have a common English word at each step.

TREE

____

____

____

____

____

STAR

Answers on page 127.

Either/Or

Complete the sentence with two words that are anagrams of each other (e.g. CARE and RACE).

Each year, Sam painstakingly _____ the colors of his outdoor Christmas _____.

Answers on page 127.

Xmas Crossword

ACROSS
1. Lose color
5. Openhanded blow
9. Anglo-___
10. Term of endearment
12. Scotch pine
15. Canned meats
16. Impolite
17. Unhappy
18. ___ Maria
19. In use
20. Bjorn ___
21. Continue despite opposition
23. Quick wash
24. Changed
26. To any extent
29. Let go
33. Tardy
34. Neat
35. Number of a Louis
36. Military mail-drop: abbr.
37. Waiter's handout
38. Do a clerk's job
39. Xmas custom
42. Vegas lights
43. School tests
44. Shower affection (on)
45. Matching pieces

DOWN
1. Food grower
2. Line of rotation
3. John ___ Passos
4. Give for safekeeping
5. Out of the sun
6. Misplace
7. Picnic pest
8. Individual
9. Use a razor
11. One's age
12. Fellow
13. Assembling, as troops
14. Border
19. Future law
20. Wait
22. Mall notice
23. Depend
25. Cuts back
26. ___ and alack
27. Make an easy putt
28. Expiated
30. Accepted truths
31. Door and window features
32. Preholiday times
34. Nervous
37. Julep garnish
38. Campus group: abbr.
40. Muck
41. Woodsman's tool

Answers on page 127.

Picture This

Place each of the 20 boxes in the 5 by 4 grid below so they form a picture of a gift holder. Do this without cutting the page apart: Use only your eyes.

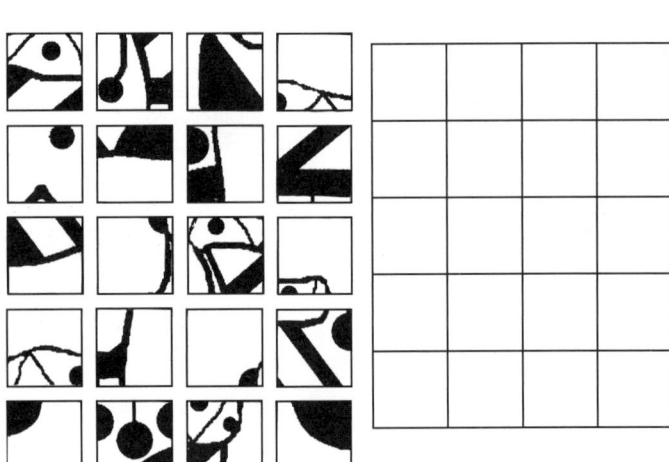

Answer on page 127.

Matching

Match each Christmas song to its singer.

1. "Santa Baby"
2. "All I Want for Christmas Is You"
3. "Blue Christmas"
4. "Last Christmas"

A. Mariah Carey
B. Wham!
C. Eartha Kitt
D. Elvis Presley

Answers on page 127.

Wassail

Cryptograms are messages in substitution code. Break the code to read the message. For example, THE SMART CAT might become FVO QWGDF JGF if F is substituted for T, V for H, O for E, and so on.

IEMMEPW, E VHR MTPLXG IPZX, IEM MEPG RH VESX HYPJPZERXG

IPRV RVX 5RV LXZRNYD WXJXZG HC RVX UXENRPCNW MEFHZ,

YHIXZE, IVH RHEMRXG RVX VXEWRV HC RVX XZJWPMV APZJ IPRV

RVX IHYGM "IEMM-VEXW!," IVPLV QXEZM "DHNY VXEWRV!"

Answer on page 128.

Gingerbread

Using the following list of clues, find words of five or six letters hidden in the word
GINGERBREAD.

1. Harass, pester _____
2. She wears white _____
3. Tight-fitting cap _____
4. Color of undyed wool _____
5. Devoid of life _____
6. Wants to please _____
7. Wish granter _____
8. Category of artistic work _____
9. Unkempt _____
10. Salted water _____
11. Novice, colloquially _____
12. "Yes, of course!" _____

Answers on page 128.

Either/Or

Complete the sentence with two words that are anagrams of each other (e.g. CARE and RACE).

Monica liked how the heels on her winter _____ gave her a _____ in height.

Answers on page 128.

It's Snow Much Fun

Change just one letter on each line to go from the top word to the bottom word. Do not change the order of the letters. You must have a common English word at each step.

SNOW

———

———

SLED

Answers on page 128.

Sleigh Ride

Using the following list of clues, find words of five or six letters hidden in the word
SLEIGH RIDE.

1. Move smoothly ____
2. Spikes and wedges ____
3. Protect ____
4. Property recipients ____
5. Avarice ____
6. Senior ____
7. Breathed sadly ____
8. Transparent ____
9. Strict ____
10. Savor or enjoy ____
11. May form a maze ____
12. Strong wish ____

Answers on page 128.

Pop Quiz

1. What year was "It's the Most Wonderful Time of the Year" recorded?

   A. 1975
   B. 1973
   C. 1963
   D. 1967

2. What is the most published Christmas hymn?

   A. "Hark! The Herald Angels Sing"
   B. "Joy to the World"
   C. "O Come, All Ye Faithful"
   D. "Silent Night"

3. How old was Brenda Lee when she recorded "Rockin' Around the Christmas Tree"?

   A. 18
   B. 21
   C. 13
   D. 15

4. "Have Yourself a Merry Little Christmas" is one of Frank Sinatra's most famous songs. But who originally recorded the classic Christmas hit?

   A. Judy Garland
   B. Bing Crosby
   C. Perry Como
   D. The Ronettes

5. What beverage does the singer tell the audience to have a cup of in "A Holly Jolly Christmas"?

   A. Happiness
   B. Hot cocoa
   C. Joy
   D. Cheer

Answers on page 128.

Answers

Pop Quiz (page 4)

B. "Account of a Visit from St. Nicholas"

Oh What Fun (page 4)

While "Jingle Bells" might be one of the most recognizable Christmas tunes of all time, the song was originally written by James Lord Pierpont to celebrate Thanksgiving. It was initially titled "The One Horse Open Sleigh."

Star Power (page 5)

O Is for Ornaments (page 6)

Answers

Bundle Up (page 8)

Answers may vary. COLD, cord, card, ward, WARM

Either/Or (page 8)

share / hears

North Pole (page 9)

Answers may vary. 1. Other; 2. honor; 3. thorn; 4. hero; 5. noel; 6. help; 7. nope; 8. poet; 9. horn; 10. hotel; 11. rope; 12. lore

Red and Green (page 10)

Matching (page 12)

1. C; 2. D; 3. A; 4. B

C_ndy _nd M_r_ (page 12)

1. Peanut brittle; 2. chocolate orange; 3. candied nuts; 4. pecan praline; 5. salted caramel; 6. chocolate truffle; 7. butter toffee; 8. caramel popcorn

Answers

Star Power (page 13)

		4	2	1		
4	1	7	★	6	3	1
3	★	8	3	5	★	2
5	6	2	★	4	7	8
8	★	7	1	6	★	5
1	4	3	★	2	1	3
		4	5	8		

The Nutcracker (page 14)

Toys for Tykes (page 16)

Answers may vary.
TRAIN, trait, tract, track, TRUCK

Either/Or (page 16)

nights / things

Santa Claus (page 17)

Answers may vary. 1. Canal; 2. lass; 3. talc; 4. sauna; 5. class; 6. scant; 7. scan; 8. tuna; 9. clan; 10. salsa; 11. cast; 12. acts

Answers

Winter Blues (page 18)

	D	A	M	S		H	A	R	M	
	R	E	M	I	T		A	L	I	A	S
P	A	L	A	C	E		S	P	O	R	T	S
O	I	L		S	T	E	T	S		I	R	E
E	L	A	L		S	O	Y		G	A	E	L
		E	T	O	N		P	E	N	A	L
	H	A	V	E	N		B	R	E	A	K
N	O	B	E	L		L	A	O	S
E	L	S	E		G	A	R		E	T	N	A
L	I	T		C	U	T	I	E		R	E	S
L	E	A	G	U	E		S	Q	U	A	S	H
	R	I	O	T	S		T	U	R	N	S
	N	A	S	T		A	I	L	S

Meet Me Under the Mistletoe (page 20)

Mistletoe plants are found almost everywhere and actually first grew in the tropics.

Pop Quiz (page 20)

C. Paris, France

Star Power (page 21)

		7	5	1		
		6	★	3		
	6	8	4	2	7	
	2	★	1	★	6	
8	5	7	3	8	5	2
3	★	4	★	1	★	3
6	1	2	5	6	7	4

Answers

P Is for Poinsettia (page 22)

```
O A L P A G M Y Q H C N U P B S
V Z E I X D T M S K S N X R U F
M P P X C R K P O S T C A R D G
H E O K A P O I N S E T T I A N
P P L P A R A D E F R L B P N I
A P A A U O N A I P S M E W P
R E B R G J G X E A A W J A R
G R E T N P A S T R I E S C L P
O M N R I Y T M W A S J F E Y S
T I O I D W L F A L R H G R V R
O N C D D N F R R S K I V U L E
H T E G U P G S T N E S E R P P
P P N E P B O D I A L P F M G I
H V I V P Y U E I P N A C E P P
H I P P O P C O R N S T R I N G
P R A N C E R L U F I T N E L P
```

Say What? (page 24)

"Christmas is love in action. Every time we love, every time we give, it's Christmas."

Under the Tree (page 24)

Answers may vary. GIFT, rift, rife, rile, PILE

Kris Kringle (page 25)

Answers may vary. 1. Girl; 2. silk; 3. skein; 4. liken; 5. rinse; 6. sink; 7. reins; 8. Erie; 9. reign; 10. rings; 11. skink; 12. rink

Answers

Skating Rink (page 26)

F	I	G	U	R	E	S	K	A	T	I	N	G
I	S	I		A	L	K	A		E	N	I	D
L	A	N	D	S	M	A	N		E	N	T	S
A	W	A	I	T		T	O	T	O			
		C	A	N	T	I	L	E	V	E	R	
N	A	M	E			A	E	R	A	T	E	
O	L	E		B	E	A	N	O		T	O	S
I	L	L	S	A	Y			C	E	N	T	
R	I	T	T	B	E	R	G	E	R			
	A	R	A	B		L	A	D	L	E		
R	O	B	O		E	A	S	T	W	O	O	D
G	U	L	L		A	H	S	O		U	R	E
B	I	E	L	L	M	A	N	N	S	P	I	N

Chr_stm_s D_nn_r (page 28)

1. Honey-glazed ham;
2. mincemeat pie; 3.
Waldorf salad; 4. mashed
potatoes; 5. roasted carrots; 6. cranberry sauce;
7. deviled eggs; 8. beef
Wellington

Matching (page 28)

1. C; 2. B; 3. D; 4. A

Star Power (page 29)

			6	3	2		
			1	★	4		
	4	8	7	5	1		
	5	★	2	★	4		
3	6	1	3	8	6	1	
4	★	2	★	5	★	3	
5	8	7	6	4	7	2	

Answers

Christmas Movies (page 30)

Either/Or (page 32)

lump / plum

Ignominious Christmas Gift (page 32)

Answers may vary. COAL, coat, coot, soot, sook, SOCK

Picture This (page 33)

Answers

Winter Flying Sport (page 34)

M	M	A		A	C	M	E		S	O	L	O
I	U	D		S	L	I	T		E	N	O	L
S	T	D		T	U	S	H		R	U	B	Y
S	T	Y	L	E	S	C	O	R	E	S		M
			A	R	T		S	A	N			P
	S	T	O	N	E	D		F	E	R	M	I
S	E	O			R	A	T			I	O	C
K	A	R	S	T		Y	O	R	U	B	A	
I		H	I	E		N	E	G				
J		L	A	N	D	I	N	G	H	I	L	L
U	S	E	D		E	L	A	N		D	O	A
M	A	G	E		M	E	G	A		L	C	M
P	L	O	D		A	X	E	L		Y	O	B

Pop Quiz (page 36)

True. In the late 1800s German crafters began making artificial Christmas trees using green-dyed goose feathers in response to deforestation concerns.

The Meaning of Eggnog (page 36)

The word "eggnog" in old English literally means "egg in a little cup."

Star Power (page 37)

		2	4	1		
		8	★	5		
	1	6	3	7	5	
	7	★	4	★	1	
2	8	5	2	8	6	7
7	★	6	★	1	★	5
1	4	3	7	4	3	2

Answers

Christmas Songs (page 38)

Say What? (page 40)

"Christmas is doing a little something extra for someone."

The Spirit of Christmas (page 40)

Answers may vary. HOPE, rope, rose, rise, wise, WISH

Joy to the World (page 41)

Answers may vary. 1. Hood; 2. trot; 3. howl; 4. yowl; 5. throw; 6. wool; 7. wrote; 8. told; 9. tooth; 10. lyre; 11. jetty; 12. dowry

Answers

Spotlight on St. Nick (page 42)

Jolabokaflod (page 44)

One popular Icelandic tradition involves exchanging new books with family members and reading them on Christmas Eve. The tradition was popularized during the Second World War, when paper was one of the few things not rationed in Iceland.

Pop Quiz (page 44)

"Jingle Bells," written in 1857, came several years before the 1864 Christmas standard, "Up on a Housetop."

Star Power (page 45)

Answers

F Is for Figgy Pudding (page 46)

Snowflake (page 49)

Answers may vary. 1. Noel; 2. fawn; 3. loaf; 4. walk; 5. sofa; 6. false; 7. swan; 8. leaf; 9. wolf; 10. alone; 11. seal; 12. aloe

Dress the Tree (page 48)

Answers may vary. TRIM, trip, drip, drop, prop, CROP

Secret Santa (page 50)

Either / Or (page 48)

note / tone

Answers

Miles and Miles of Christmas Cheer (page 52)

Holiday Tree Farms in Corvallis, Oregon, is one of the largest Christmas tree farms in the world. On average, they ship out about a million trees per year.

Merry and BRIGHT (page 53)

The famous Rockefeller Christmas Tree in New York City is lit with over fifty thousand LED lights, which is over five miles of wire.

Matching (page 52)

1. B; 2. C; 3. A; 4. D

Pop Quiz (page 53)

D. 1943

Gifts Handmade with Love (page 54)

Answers

Star Power (page 56)

A Holiday Hoard! (page 57)

Answers may vary. GIFT, gilt, tilt, till, tile, PILE

Either / Or (page 57)

coast / coats

Hiding Some Christmas Things (page 58)

F	A	T	E		M	E	S	S		D	R	A	M	A
O	L	A	V		E	R	I	E		O	U	T	E	R
P	E	T	E		M	A	R	L		C	R	O	S	S
	C	A	R	L	O	S	S	A	N	T	A	N	A	
			G	O	R	E			A	O	L			
S	H	E	R	R	Y		U	S	S	R		B	A	M
E	E	L	E	D		A	S	E	A		S	O	L	I
A	C	C	E	S	S	H	O	L	L	Y	W	O	O	D
T	H	I	N		H	O	F	F		O	A	T	H	S
O	E	D		H	I	Y	A		S	U	N	H	A	T
			K	O	S			F	O	L	K			
	N	O	R	T	H	C	A	R	O	L	I	N	A	
M	A	C	A	O		A	L	O	T		E	A	S	E
E	T	H	A	N		P	O	S	H		S	N	I	T
T	O	O	L	E		T	E	T	E			T	O	A	D

Drummer Boy (page 60)

Answers may vary. 1. Robe; 2. body; 3. bored; 4. merry; 5. order; 6. obey; 7. berry; 8. rummy; 9. demo; 10. dour; 11. ruby; 12. rumor

Answers

Matching (page 61)

1. C; 2. B; 3. D; 4. A

M_d_rn S_ng_rs (page 61)

1. Kacey Musgraves; 2. Mariah Carey; 3. Justin Bieber; 4. Ariana Grande; 5. Sufjan Stevens; 6. Kelly Clarkson; 7. Michael Bublé; 8. Carly Rae Jepsen

On the Nice List (page 62)

Star Power (page 64)

Answers

Winter Fun (page 65)

Answers may vary.
SNOW, show, shop, ship, skip, SKIS

Either / Or (page 65)

silent / tinsel

Christmas at the Movies (page 66)

Picture This (page 68)

Pop Quiz (page 69)

B. "Tinkle Bells"

Answers

Kalle Anka (page 69)

On Christmas Eve in Sweden, almost half the country sits down at three in the afternoon to watch a Donald Duck Christmas special that airs every year.

Star Power (page 72)

N Is for Noel (page 70)

Sleigh Bells Ring (page 73)

Answers may vary. BELL, bill, will, wild, wind, wing, RING

Answers

Say What? (page 73)

"He who has not Christmas in his heart will never find it under a tree."

Christmas Tunes (page 74)

G	L	A	M		S	C	U	D		S	I	M	B	A
R	A	N	I		T	U	B	E		E	T	O	Y	S
E	S	T	S		U	S	E	S		N	E	N	E	H
W	H	I	T	E	C	H	R	I	S	T	M	A	S	
			L	A	C	Y			H	R	S			
L	I	K	E	S	O		A	R	I	A		T	R	U
U	N	I	T	E		A	L	A	N		R	A	I	N
C	A	R	O	L	O	F	T	H	E	B	E	L	L	S
E	L	B	E		U	T	E	S		E	V	O	K	E
S	L	Y		C	Z	A	R		E	V	E	N	E	R
			A	Y	E		D	U	E	L				
	J	I	N	G	L	E	B	E	L	L	R	O	C	K
R	O	D	I	N		R	O	T	O		I	S	O	N
M	E	E	S	E		R	O	E	G		E	L	L	E
S	L	E	E	T		S	P	R	Y		S	O	M	E

Mistletoe (page 76)

Answers may vary. 1. Motel; 2. smile; 3. stole; 4. title; 5. slime; 6. moist; 7. mettle; 8. omelet; 9. mottle; 10. islet; 11. toils; 12. totem

Matching (page 77)

1. C; 2. D; 3. A; 4. B

Answers

Th_ Cl_ss_cs (page 77)

1. Nat King Cole; 2. Dean Martin; 3. Bing Crosby; 4. Burl Ives; 5. Ella Fitzgerald; 6. Darlene Love; 7. Gene Autry; 8. Louis Armstrong

Star Power (page 80)

2	8	3				
	4	★	6	7	2	
3	1	7	5	★	4	6	7
6	★	4	3	1	8	★	1
2	8	5	★	7	2	3	5
	2	6	8	★	1	
		5	6	4		

Christmas Critters (page 78)

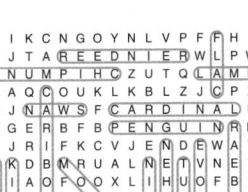

Festive and Toasty (page 81)

Answers may vary. YULE, mule, mole, mope, mops, lops, LOGS

Either / Or (page 81)

reveals / several

Answers

Deck the Halls (page 82)

B	O	A	R		L	A	T	T	E		R	O	N	I
I	N	R	I		A	N	G	E	L		O	F	I	T
L	E	O	N		S	T	I	C	K		A	F	L	Y
B	O	U	G	H	S	O	F	H	O	L	L	Y		
O	U	S			E	O	N			I	D	O	N	T
S	T	E	I	N			M	I	E	N		U	A	R
		D	I	A	R	I	S	T		A	G	C	Y	
		Y	U	L	E	T	I	D	E	C	A	R	O	L
M	I	T	E		R	O	S	E	H	I	P			
G	P	A		M	A	S	T			T	S	K	E	D
M	E	H	T	A			M	I	C		E	D	E	
		J	O	I	N	T	H	E	C	H	O	R	U	S
O	M	A	R		A	W	A	R	E		I	N	C	A
D	A	Z	S		V	A	L	L	I		S	E	E	D
O	R	Z	O		E	S	S	E	N		E	L	S	E

Pop Quiz (page 85)

A. Mulled punch, often with oranges and apples

Sleigh Ride (page 85)

The image of Santa Claus flying his sleigh was created in the early nineteenth century by Washington Irving—the same author who dreamt up the Headless Horseman.

Picture This (page 84)

Answers

Santa's Sleigh (page 86)

Star Power (page 88)

Stay Warm (page 89)

Answers may vary. COZY, copy, cope, core, wore, wire, FIRE

Say What? (page 89)

"When we recall Christmas past, we usually find that the simplest things—not the great occasions—give off the greatest glow of happiness."

Answers

Holiday Traditions (page 90)

On the Naughty List (page 92)

Answers may vary. 1. Saint; 2. shiny; 3. satin; 4. giant; 5. signal; 6. sunlit; 7. night; 8. guilty; 9. laugh; 10. light; 11. lying; 12. shanty

Pop Quiz (page 93)

C. "O Tannenbaum"

New Popular Christmas Treat (page 93)

Christmas candies run the gamut from fudge to taffy and everything in between, but peppermint bark has become a favorite in modern times.

Santa and Company (page 94)

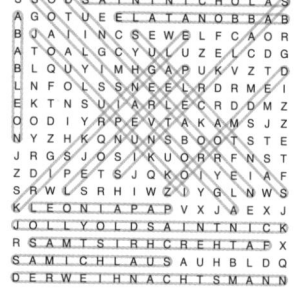

Answers

Star Power (page 96)

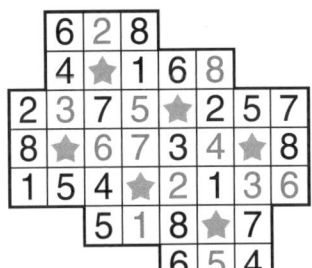

Xmas Crossword (page 98)

Tree Topper (page 97)

Answers may vary. TREE, thee, them, teem, team, tear, sear, STAR

Picture This (page 100)

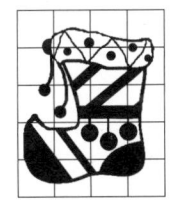

Either/Or (page 97)

coordinates/decorations

Matching (page 101)

1. C; 2. A; 3. D; 4. B

Answers

Wassail (page 101)

Wassail, a hot spiced wine, was said to have originated with the 5th century legend of the beautiful Saxon, Rowena, who toasted the health of the English king with the words "wass-hael!," which means "your health!"

Gingerbread (page 102)

Answers may vary. 1. Badger; 2. bride; 3. beanie; 4. beige; 5. barren; 6. eager; 7. genie; 8. genre; 9. ragged; 10. brine; 11. green; 12. agree

Either/Or (page 103)

boots/boost

It's Snow Much Fun (page 103)

Answers may vary. SNOW, slow, slew, SLED

Sleigh Ride (page 104)

Answers may vary. 1. Glide; 2. heels; 3. shield; 4. heirs; 5. greed; 6. elder; 7. sighed; 8. sheer; 9. rigid; 10. relish; 11. hedge; 12. desire

Pop Quiz (page 105)

1. C; 2. B; 3. C; 4. A; 5. D